T0210059

EVERLASTING

—— TO ——

EVERLASTING

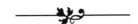

GOD CHANGE NOT:
MALACHI 3:6

LARRY DEVOE

authorHOUSE®

AuthorHouse™
1663 Liberty Drive
Bloomington, IN 47403
www.authorhouse.com
Phone: 1 (800) 839-8640

Published by AuthorHouse 02/08/2019

ISBN: 978-1-5462-7856-6 (sc)
ISBN: 978-1-5462-7987-7 (e)

Print information available on the last page.

Any people depicted in stock imagery provided by Getty Images are models,
and such images are being used for illustrative purposes only.
Certain stock imagery © Getty Images.

This book is printed on acid-free paper.

Because of the dynamic nature of the Internet, any web addresses or
links contained in this book may have changed since publication and
may no longer be valid. The views expressed in this work are solely those
of the author and do not necessarily reflect the views of the publisher,
and the publisher hereby disclaims any responsibility for them.

Scripture quotations marked KJV are from the Holy Bible, King James Version
(Authorized Version). First published in 1611. Quoted from the KJV Classic
Reference Bible, Copyright © 1983 by The Zondervan Corporation.

Scripture quotations marked AMP are from The Amplified Bible, Old
Testament copyright © 1965, 1987 by the Zondervan Corporation. The
Amplified Bible, New Testament copyright © 1954, 1958, 1987 by
The Lockman Foundation. Used by permission. All rights reserved.

PREFACE

Scriptures from the Holy Bible; God's Word: and precepts for us to live by; on how to know God our Father in heaven and have a personal relationship with Him through our Lord and Savior Jesus Christ.

GOD EVERLASTING TO EVERLASTING

God does not change. God is the Creator of all things in heaven, the universe everything in it including earth; everything in and on earth. God Created mankind to be His people He their God, God given everyone a brain [along with] two most important choices of their lives; follow the Spirit; feel peace from heaven [along with] guidance and direction; fulfilling God's will for your life. The other choice is follow the lusts of the flesh. God allows circumstances in your life to get your attention due to the fact God predestined our lives long before conception. Known unto God are all his works from the beginning of the world [Acts 15:18 KJV]. The Bible is God's Word for us to live by. Everything from God's precepts wisdom and understanding is in the Bible. God's Word came to prophets written books in the old testament. Lord Jesus Christ appeared to apostles after His resurrection written books in the new testament. For my thoughts are not your thoughts, neither are your ways my ways saith the Lord. For as the heavens are higher than the earth, so are my ways higher than your ways, and my than your thoughts. [Isa. 55:7,8 KJV]. There are those who think God [is

1

a myth], while they cherish things in the flesh. Who changed the truth of God into a lie, and worshipped and served the creature more than the Creator, who is blessed for ever, Amen.[Rom. 1:25 KJV]. I read the Bible and stand strong in God's Word, also observe current events in the world today, noticing how God's Word in the Bible is consistently fulfilling. The population and technology of the earth in the Bible days were not nearly as it is today; God Who knows all things. God said; it shall come to pass I will pour out my Spirit upon all flesh: and your sons and your daughters shall prophesy, and your young men shall see visions, and your old men shall dream dreams: [Joel 2:28, Acts 2:17 KJV]. Those of us heard sermons and read about having a personal relationship with God. Now the God of hope fill you with all joy and peace in believing, that ye may abound in hope, through the power of the Holy Ghost. [Rom. 15:13 KJV]. Some of us heard sayings; God is on our side, God is with us. Some of us have had our own personal experience that we know only God through our Lord and Savior Jesus Christ can accomplish in our lives. When we have God's Holy Spirit in us, we want to practice God's precepts; we want to read and stand strong in God's Word nourishing our spirit enjoying everyday life with the Holy Spirit of God in Christ dwells with our spirit in us. Our Lord Jesus Christ said [in John 3:6 KJV] That is born of the flesh is flesh; and that is born of the Spirit is spirit. For God so loved the world, that He gave His only begotten Son, that whosoever believeth in him should not perish, but have everlasting life. For God sent not his Son into the world to condemn the world; but that the world through him might be saved.[John 3:16,17 KJV]. Through Lord Jesus Christ [Whom] God given everything, is our only way to pray to God, [Father I come to You in the Name of Jesus] communications with God is open.

REFLECTION:

_____

_____

_____

_____

_____

_____

_____

_____

_____

_____

_____

_____

_____

_____

_____

_____

_____

_____

_____

_____

_____

_____

At the name of Jesus every knee shall bow, of things in heaven, and things in earth, and things under the earth; And that every tongue shall confess that Jesus Christ is Lord, to the glory of God the Father.[Phl 2:10,11 KJV]. God given all authority over to His Son our Lord and Savior Jesus Christ [Whom] defeated satan at the cross when He descended before His resurrection on the third day: Therefore satan himself also shall bow at the name of Jesus and confess Jesus Christ is Lord to the glory of God our Father in heaven. Sometimes there is tension in our lives that we must resist due to the fact it is only negative energy from the evil prince of this world. For we wrestle not against flesh and blood, but against principalities, against powers, against the rulers of the darkness of this world, against spiritual wickedness in high places.[Eph. 6:12 KJV]. Put on the whole armour of God, that ye may be able to stand against the wiles of the devil.[Eph. 6:11 KJV]. Therefore we must walk in the Holy Spirit Whom gives peace beyond understanding the human mind cannot comprehend. When our Lord and Savior Jesus Christ nailed to the cross said to Father God in heaven, it is finished; sins of the world were forgiven. The only thing you must do is resist all tension and negative energy that is not of God's Holy Spirit: [unless God want your attention allowing circumstances to occur in your life], relax in God's peace from heaven that will guide you and direct you unto God's will for your life and you will enjoy everyday life here on earth and eternal life with Father God in heaven. God that made the world and all things therein, seeing that he is Lord of heaven and earth, dwelleth not in temples made with hands; Neither is worshipped with men's hands,as though he needed any thing, seeing he giveth to all life, and breath, and all things; And hath made of one blood all nations of men for to dwell on all the face of the earth, and hath determined the times before appointed,and the bounds of their habitation; That they should seek the Lord, if haply they might feel after him, and find him, though he be not far from every one of us:[Act 17:24-27 KJV]. When we seek the Kingdom of heaven although we know God lives in all who are His: even your subconscious mind is programmed to truth, wisdom and knowledge from God through Christ; due to the fact Jesus said in [Luke 18:27 KJV] The things which are impossible with men are possible with God. But ye are not in the flesh, but in the Spirit, if so be that the Spirit of God dwell in you. Now if any man have not the Spirit of Christ, he is none of his. [Rom. 8:9 KJV]. Many of us who are led by and walk in the Spirit of God are the sons of God thanks to our Lord and Savior Jesus Christ Who shed His blood for many to received the Holy Spirit. Likewise the Spirit also helpeth our infirmities: for we know not what we should pray for as we ought: but the Spirit itself maketh intercession for us with groanings which cannot be uttered. And he that searcheth the hearts knoweth what is the mind of the Spirit, because he maketh intercession for the saints according to the will of God.[Rom. 8:26,27 KJV].

REFLECTION:

_____
_____
_____
_____
_____
_____
_____
_____
_____
_____
_____
_____
_____
_____
_____
_____
_____
_____
_____
_____
_____

Those of us who read God's Word; know all about His covenant with Abraham; God's Word came to the prophets in many forms. God appeared to Moses written the first five books in the old testament of the bible which includes the laws and commandments and precepts of God. God knows all things; predestined His Word is comprehend around the earth before His Son; our Lord and Savior Jesus Christ return in the manner He was taken up; now is seated at the right hand of Father God in heaven. Set your affection on things above, not on things on the earth. For ye are dead, and your life is hid with Christ in God.[Col.3:2,3 KJV]. Let the word of Christ dwell in you richly in all wisdom; some of us strong in the Spirit of God in Christ continuously giving thanks to God our Father in heaven. God's Word through our Lord and Savior Jesus Christ is the second covenant; God predestined because God knows all things before transpiration. In the Holy Bible, God's Word for us to live by; there is power and wisdom and strength and riches and honour and glory and blessings and faith; our Lord Jesus Christ is the author and finisher of faith. Faith is not what God can do for you; faith is what God have done for you according to His will for your life. You can apply the power of God's Word to your everyday life; you receive wisdom; the fear of God is the beginning of all wisdom, There is one Spirit, even as many are called;

One Lord, one faith, one baptism, One God and Father of all; since we have gone from being servants of God to children of God when our Lord and Savior Jesus Christ nailed to the cross and shed blood for all; also the propitiation for the sins of the world. Let the word of Christ dwell in you richly in all wisdom; teaching and admonishing one another in psalms and hymns and spiritual songs, singing with grace in your hearts to the Lord. And whatever ye do in word or deed, do all in the name of the Lord Jesus, giving thanks to God the Father by him.[Col.3:16,17 KJV]. For the word of God is quick, and powerful, and sharper than any twoedged sword, piercing even to the dividing asunder of soul and spirit, and of the joints and marrow, is a discerner of the thoughts and intents of the heart.[Heb.4:12 KJV]. Let us hear the conclusion of the whole matter: Fear God, and keep his commandments: for this is the whole duty of man. For God shall bring every work into judgment, with every secret thing, whether it be good, or whether it be evil. For we know that if our earthly house of this tabernacle were dissolved, we have a building of God, an house not made with hands, eternal in the heavens. [2 Cor.5:1 KJV]. (For we walk by faith, not by sight:) [2 Cor.5:7 KJV]. And all things are of God, who hath reconciled us to himself by Jesus Christ, and hath given us the ministry of reconciliation; To wit, that God was in

Christ, reconciling the world unto himself, not imputing their trespasses unto them; and hath committed unto us the word of reconciliation.[2 Cor.5:18,19 KJV]. Let your moderation be known unto all men. The Lord is at hand. Be careful for nothing; but in every thing by prayer and supplication with thanksgiving let your requests be made known unto God.[Phi.4:5,6 KJV].

REFLECTION:

_____

_____

_____

_____

_____

_____

_____

_____

_____

_____

_____

_____

_____

_____

_____

_____

_____

_____

_____

_____

_____

_____

Be sober, be vigilant; because your adversary the devil, as a roaring lion, walketh about, seeking whom he may devour; Whom resist stedfast in faith, knowing that the same afflictions are accomplished in your brethren that are in the world.[1Ptr. 5:8,9 KJV]. Most of us see and hear daily current events from local to international and beyond the earth's atmosphere. Some of us have heard people say the devil is busy, that don't phase those of us who resist all evil and wicked temptation of the adversary. Those of us know God cannot be tempted with evil, neither tempt no man. Every man is tempted when he is enticed because of his own lusts of the flesh. Thou believest that there is one God; thou doest well: the devils also believe, and tremble.[James 2:19 KJV]. Yes of course the devil himself tremble at the name of Jesus. Call on the name Jesus the powerful Name of our Lord and Savior: the adversary will tremble. God put the enemy under His footstool. Submit yourselves therefore to God, Resist the devil, and he will flee from you. [James 4:7 KJV]. Draw near to God and He will return to you. Relax in God's peace from heaven; not peace of this world that can lead to fear or a troubled heart. In the world today God knows from creation; modern technology, enormous amount of verbal inordinateness that can be resisted by those who are born in the Spirit of God. Let the mind be in you which was also in Christ

Jesus: When adversity occur; take a moment to think, ask yourself "what would Jesus say or do under these circumstances?" Those who read comprehend and stand strong in God's Word; relaxing and walking in the Holy Spirit of God through Christ shine as lights in the world. Thou therefore endure hardness, as a good soldier of Jesus Christ. No man that warreth entangleth himself with the affairs of this life; that he may please him who chosen him to be a soldier,[2 Tim .2:3,4 KJV]. When you endure and there is peace in your subconscious mind; follow that peace that lead you with a positive response towards all adversity. There is therefore now no condemnation to them which are in Christ Jesus, who walk not after the flesh, but after the Spirit. For the law of the Spirit of life in Christ Jesus hath made me from the law of sin and death. That the righteousness of the law might be fulfilled in us, who walk not after the flesh, but after the Spirit.[Rom. 8:1,2,4 KJV]. Likewise the Spirit also helpeth our infirmities: for we know not what we should pray for as we ought: but the Spirit itself maketh intercession for us with groanings which cannot be uttered. And he that searcheth the hearts knoweth what is the mind of the Spirit, because he maketh intercession for the saints according to the will of God.[Rom. 8: 26,27 KJV]. Beloved brothers and sisters in Christ, we all have to endure at times, there are some people have to verbalize their entities. If you have to verbalize; direct it to the adversary telling evil to back away from you by the authority of the Name of Jesus: the most powerful name in heaven and earth: satan and all of his evil and wickedness tremble at the Name of Jesus. It is much easier to be quiet and resist the devil and his temptation, and he will flee from you. Always remember the adversary who tremble at the Name of Jesus must also shall bow at the Name of Jesus.

REFLECTION:

Some of us have heard that the universe can bring things to earth; there is One higher than the universe. There are those who live by their circumstances, saying I can't because: they should shed the negative energy due to the fact it is not from God Who is above and through the universe and here on earth dwelling in all of us that are born of God's Holy Spirit poured upon all flesh. I can do all things through Christ Jesus which strengtheneth me.[Phi. 4:13 KJV]. But God shall supply all your need according to his riches in glory by Christ Jesus. Now unto God and our Father be glory for ever and ever. Amen.[Phi. 4:19,20 KJV]. Those of us have learned to seek God and the kingdom of heaven first: and all things added upon us. Set your affection on things above, not things on the earth. For ye are dead, and and your life is hid with Christ in God.[Col.3:2,3 KJV]. But now ye also must put off all anger wrath, malice blasphemy, filthy communication, and lie not one to another because all liars shall not enter the kingdom of heaven. Put on the new man, which is renewed in knowledge after the image of him that created him[Col.3:10 KJV]. I know that we cannot see past the universe. God created the universe; poured His Spirit upon all flesh on the earth. When God rain down blessings upon those who are His due to the fact God lives and dwell in all who are His. Ye are of God, little children, and have overcome them: because greater is he that in you, than he that is in the world. They are of the world: therefore speak they the world, and the world heareth them.[1 John 4:4,5 KJV]. No man hath seen God at any time. If we love one another, God dwelleth in us, and his love is perfected in us. Hereby know that we dwell in him, and he in us, because he hath given us of his Spirit.[1 John 4:12,13 KJV]. Forasmuch then as Christ hath suffered for us in the flesh, arm yourselves likewise with the same mind: for he that hath suffered in the flesh hath ceased from sin; That he no longer should live the rest of his time in the flesh to the lusts of men, but to the will of God.[1 Pet.4:1,2 KJV]. If any man speak, let him speak as the oracles of God; if any man minister, let him do it as of the ability which God giveth: that God in all things may be glorified through Jesus Christ, to whom be praise and dominion for ever and ever. Amen.[1 Pet.4:11 KJV]. Wherefore let them that suffer according to the will of God commit the keeping of their souls to him in well doing, as unto a faithful Creator. [1 Pet.4:19 KJV]. The Lord executeth righteousness and judgment for all that are oppressed. He made known his ways unto Moses, his acts unto the children of Israel. The Lord is merciful and gracious, slow to anger, and plenteous in mercy. He will not always chide: neither will he keep his anger for ever.[Psalms 103:6-9 KJV]. But the mercy of the Lord is from everlasting to everlasting upon them that fear him, and his righteousness unto children's children;

To such as keep his covenant, and to those that remember his commandments to do them. The Lord hath prepared his throne in the heavens; and his kingdom ruleth over all. [Psalms 103:17-19 KJV].

REFLECTION:

_____
_____
_____
_____
_____
_____
_____
_____
_____
_____
_____
_____
_____
_____
_____
_____
_____
_____
_____
_____
_____
_____

Our Lord and Savior Jesus Christ knowing that the Father had given all things into his hands, and that he was come from God, and went to God;[John 13:3 KJV]. The kingdom of God is from everlasting to everlasting and have no end. God did not appoint us to wrath, but to obtain salvation by our Lord Jesus Christ, Who died for us, that whether we wake or sleep, we should live together with and in Him. Therefore we are buried with him by baptism into death: that like as Christ was raised up from the dead by the glory of the Father, even so we also should walk in newness of life. For if we have been planted together in the likeness of his death, we shall be also in the likeness of his resurrection: [Rom.6:4,5 KJV]. According as he hath chosen us in him before the foundation of the world, that we should be holy and without blame before him in love: Having predestined us unto the adoption of children by Jesus Christ to himself, according to the good pleasure of his will: In whom we have redemption through his blood, the forgiveness of sins, according to the riches of his grace; Wherein he hath abounded toward us in all wisdom and prudence; Having made known unto us the mystery of his will, according to his good pleasure he hath purposed in himself: That in the dispensation of the fulness of times he might gather together in one all things in Christ, both which are in heaven, and which are on earth; even in him. [Eph.1:4,5,7-10 KJV]. There is one body, and one Spirit, even as ye are called in one hope of your calling; One Lord, one faith, one baptism, One God and Father of all, who is above all and through all, in you all. But unto every one of us is given grace according to the measure of the gift of Christ. Wherefore he saith, When he ascended up on high, he led captivity captive, and gave gifts to men. Now that he ascended, what is it but that he also he also descended first into the lower parts of the earth? He that descended is the same also that ascended up far above all heavens, that he might fill all things.[Eph.4:4-10 KJV]. Submit yourselves therefore to God. Resist the devil, and he will flee from you.[James 4:7 KJV]. Blessed are the undefiled in the way, who walk in the law of the Lord. Blessed are they that keep his testimonies, and that seek him with the whole heart. They also do no iniquity: they walk in his ways. Thou hast commanded us to keep thy precepts diligently. [Psalms,119:1-4 KJV]. But unto them which are called, both Jews and Greeks, Christ he power of God, and the wisdom of God. Because of foolishness of God is wiser than men; and the weakness of God is stronger than men. For ye see your calling, brethren, how that not many wise men after the flesh, not many mighty, not many noble, are called: But God hath chosen the foolish things of the world to confound the wise; and God hath chosen the weak things of the world to confound the things which are mighty; And base things of the world, and things which are despised, hath God chosen, yea, and things which are not, to bring to nought things that are: That no flesh should glory in his presence. But of him are ye in Christ Jesus, who of God is made unto us wisdom, and righteousness, and sanctification, and redemption: That, according as it is written, He that glorieth, let him glory in the Lord.[1 Cor.1:24-31 KJV]

REFLECTION:

_____
_____
_____
_____
_____
_____
_____
_____
_____
_____
_____
_____
_____
_____
_____
_____
_____
_____
_____
_____
_____
_____

God created His people to give all praise and glory and worship our God and Father in heaven. Blessed be the God and Father of our Lord Jesus Christ, which according to his abundant mercy hath begotten us again unto lively hope by the resurrection of Jesus Christ from the dead, To an inheritance incorruptible, and undefiled, and fadeth not away, reserved in heaven for you, Who are kept by the power of God through faith unto salvation ready to be revealed in the last time.[1 Pet.1:3-5 KJV]. That the trial of your faith, being much more precious than of gold that perisheth, though it be tried with fire, might be found unto praise and honour and glory at the appearing of Jesus Christ: Whom having not seen. Ue love; in whom. Though now ye see him not, yet believing, ye rejoice with joy unspeakable and full of glory: Receiving the end of your faith, even the salvation of your souls, Wherefore gird up the loins of your mind, be sober, and hope to the end for the grace that is to be brought unto you at the revelation of Jesus Christ; as obedient children, not fashioning yourselves according to the former lusts in your ignorance: Forasmuch as ye know that ye were not redeemed with corruptible things, as silver and gold, from your vain conversation received by the tradition from your fathers; But with the precious blood of Christ, as of a lamb without blemish and without spot: Who verify was foreordained before the foundation of the world, but was manifest in these last times for you, Who by him do believe in God, that raised him up from the dead, and gave him glory; that your faith and hope might be in God. Being born again, not of corruptible seed, but of incorruptible, by the word of God, which liveth and abideth for ever.[1 Pet.1:7-23 KJV]. And if Christ be in you, the body is dead because of sin; but the Spirit is life because of righteousness. But if the Spirit of him that raised up Jesus from the dead dwell in you, he that raised up Christ from the dead shall also quicken your mortal bodies by his Spirit that dwelleth in you. For as many as are led by the Spirit of God, they are the sons of God. For ye have not received the spirit of bondage again to fear; but ye have received the Spirit of adoption, whereby we cry, Abba, Father. The Spirit itself beareth witness with our spirit, that we are the children of God: And if children, then heirs; heirs of God, and joint-heirs with Christ; if so be that we suffer with him, that we may be also glorified together. Likewise the Spirit also helpeth our infirmities: for we know not what we should pray for as we ought: but the Spirit itself maketh intercession for us with groanings which cannot be uttered. And he that searcheth the hearts knoweth what is the mind of the Spirit, because he maketh intercession for the saints according to the will of God. What shall we then say to these things? If

God be for us, who can be against us? He that spared not his own Son, but delivered him up for us all, how shall he not with him also freely give us all things? [Rom.8:10,11,14-17,26,27,31,32 KJV].

REFLECTION:

_____
_____
_____
_____
_____
_____
_____
_____
_____
_____
_____
_____
_____
_____
_____
_____
_____
_____
_____
_____
_____
_____

There is one lawgiver, who is able to save and to destroy: who art thou that judgest another?[James 4:12 KJV]. And grieve not the holy Spirit of God, whereby ye are sealed unto the day of redemption. Let all bitterness and wrath, and anger, and clamour, and evil speaking, be put away from you, with all malice: And be ye kind to another, tenderhearted, forgiving one another, even as God for Christ's sake hath forgiven you,[Eph.4:30-32 KJV]. And what is the exceeding greatness of his power to us-ward who believe, according to the working of his mighty power, Which he wrought in Christ, when he raised him from the dead, and set him at his own fight hand in the heavenly places, Far above all principality, and power, and might, and dominion, and every name that is named, not only in this world, but also in that which is to come: And hath put all things under his feet, and gave him to be the head over all things to the church, Which is his body, the fullness of him that filleth all in all.[Eph.1:19-23 KJV]. But God who is rich in mercy, for his great love wherewith he loved us, Even when we were dead in sins, hath quickened us together with Christ, (by grace ye are saved;) And hath raised us up together, and made us sit together in heavenly places in Christ Jesus: That in the ages to come he might show the exceeding riches of his grace in his kindness toward us through Christ Jesus. For by grace are ye saved through faith; and that not of yourselves: it is the gift of God: Not of works, lest any man should boast. For we are his workmanship, created in Christ Jesus unto good works, which God hath before ordained that we should walk in them. But now in Christ Jesus ye who sometimes were far off are made nigh by the blood of Christ. For he is our peace who hath made both one, and broken down the middle wall of partition between us; Having abolished in his flesh the enmity, even the law of commandments contained in ordinances; for to make in himself of twain one new man, so making peace; And that he might reconcile both unto God in one body by the cross, having slain the enmity thereby: For through him we both have access by one Spirit unto the Father.[Eph.2:13-16,18 KJV]. And all things are of God, who hath reconciled us to himself by Jesus Christ, and hath given to us the ministry of reconciliation; To wit, that God was in Christ, reconciling the world unto himself, not imputing their trespasses unto them; and hath committed unto us the word of reconciliation. For he hath made him to be sin for us, who knew no sin; that we might be made the righteousness of God in him.[2 Cor.5:18,19,21 KJV]. For the wrath of God is revealed from heaven against all ungodliness and unrighteousness of men, who hold the truth in unrighteousness; Because that which may known of God is manifest in them; for God hath shewed it unto them. For the invisible things of him from the creation of the world are clearly seen, being understood by the things that are made, even his eternal power and Godhead; so that they are without excuse: Because that, when they knew God, they glorified him not as God, neither were thankful; but became vain in their imaginations, and their foolish heart was darkened. [Rom.1:18,19-21 KJV].

REFLECTION:

_____

_____

_____

_____

_____

_____

_____

_____

_____

_____

_____

_____

_____

_____

_____

_____

_____

_____

_____

_____

And be not conformed to this world: but be ye transformed by the renewing of your mind, that ye may prove what is that good, and acceptable, and perfect, will of God. For we have many members in one body, and all members have not the same office: So we, being many, are one body in Christ, and every one members one of another. Let love be without dissimulation. Abhor that which is evil; cleave to that which is good. Be of the same mind one toward another. Mind not high things, but condescend to men of low estate. Be not wise in your own conceits. Recompense to no man evil for evil. Provide things honest in the sight of all men. If it be possible, as much as lieth in you, live peaceably with all men. Dearly beloved, avenge not yourselves, but rather give place unto wrath: for it is written, Vengeance is mine; I will repay, saith the Lord. Therefore if thine enemy hunger, feed him; if he thirst, give him drink: for in so doing thou shalt heap coals of fire on his head. Be not overcome of evil, but overcome evil with good.[Rom.12:4,5,9,16-21 KJV]. The time our Lord and Savior Jesus Christ was walking in this world in the flesh descended from the seed of Abraham and the holy Spirit of God: whom God through the prophets communicated with the seeds of Abraham written books in the old testament of the bible. Jesus said; judge not, that ye be not judged. For with what judgment ye judged, ye shall be judged: and with what measure ye mete, it shall

33

be measured to you again. Ask, and it shall be given you; seek, and ye shall find; knock,and it shall be opened unto you: For every one that asketh receiveth; and he that seek findeth; and to him that knocketh it shall be opened. [Mat.7:1,2,7,8 KJV]. For many deceivers are entered into the world, who confess not that Jesus Christ is come in the flesh. This is a deceiver and an antichrist.[2 John.1:7 KJV]. Walk in the Spirit, and ye shall not fulfil the lust of the flesh. For the flesh lusteth against the Spirit, and the Spirit against the flesh: and these are contrary the one to the other: so that ye cannot do the things that ye would.[Gal.5:16,17 KJV]. Wherefore whosoever shal eat this bread, and drink this cup of the Lord, unworthy, shall be guilty of the body and blood of the Lord. But let a man examine himself, and so let him eat of that bread and drink of that cup. For he that eateth and drinketh unworthy, eateth and drinketh damnation to himself, not discerning the Lord's body. For this cause many are weak and sickly among you, and sleep. For if we would judge ourselves, we should not be judged. But when we are judged, we are chastened of the Lord, that we should not be condemned with the world.[1 Cor.11:27-32 KJV]. True worshippers shall worship the Father in spirit and in truth: for the Father seeketh such to worship him. Dod is a Spirit: and they that worship him must worship him in spirit and in truth,[John 4:23,24 KJV]. Those of us that do truth are lights in the world and our deeds may be made made manifest. That they are carefully formed or worked in God in heaven and in us through our Lord and Savior Jesus Christ. God that made the world and all things therein, seeing that he is Lord of heaven and earth, dwelleth not in temples made with hands; Neither is worshipped with men's hands, as though he needed any thing, seeing he giveth all life, and breath, and all things; And hath made of one blood all nations of men for to dwell on all the face of the earth, and hath determined the times before appointed, and the bounds of their habitation; that they should seek the Lord, if haply they might feel after him, and find him, though he be not far from every one of us: For in him we live, and move, and have our being; as certain also of your own poets have said, For we are also his offspring.[Acts 17:24-28 KJV].

REFLECTION:

The Lord is slow to anger, and great in power, and will not at all acquit the wicked: the Lord hath his way in the whirlwind and in the storm, and the clouds are the dust of his feet.[Nah.1:3 KJV]. **Behold, the nations are as a drop of a bucket, and are counted as the small dust of the balance: behold, he taketh up the isles as as very little thing. All nations before him are as nothing; and they are counted to him less than nothing, and vanity. To whom then will ye liken God? Or what likeness will ye compare unto him? The workman melteth a graven image, the goldsmith spreadeth it over with gold, and cast silver chains. He that is so impoverished that he hath no oblation chooseth a tree that will not rot; he seeketh unto him a cunning workman to prepare a graven image, that shall not be moved. Have ye not known? Have ye not heard? Hath it not been told you from the beginning? Have ye not understood from the foundations of the earth? It is he that sitteth upon the circle of the earth, and the inhabitants thereof are as grasshoppers; that stretcheth out the heavens as a curtain, and spreadeth them out as a tent to dwell in: That bringeth the princes to nothing; he maketh the judges of the earth as vanity. Yea, they shall be planted; yea, they shall not be sown: yea their stock shall not take root in the earth: and he also blow upon them, and they shall wither, and the whirlwind shall** take them away as stubble. To whom then will ye liken me,or shall I be equal? Saith the Holy One. Lift up your eyes on high, and behold who hath created these things, that bringeth out their host by number: he calleth them all by names by the greatness of his might, for that he is strong in power; not one faileth. Why sayest thou, O Jacob, and speakest, O Israel, My way is hid from the LORD, and my judgment is passed over from my God? Hast thou not known? Hast thou not heard, that the everlasting God, the LORD, the Creator of the ends of the earth, fainteth not, neither is weary? There is no searching of his understanding,[Isa.40:15,17-28 KJV]. Thou shalt not make unto thee any graven image, or any likeness of any thing that is in heaven above, or that is in the earth beneath, or that is in the water under the earth: Thou shalt not bow down thyself to them, nor serve them: for I the LORD thy God am a jealous God, visiting the iniquity of the fathers upon the children unto the third and fourth generation of them that hate me: And shewing mercy unto thousands of them that love me, and keep my commandments. Thou shalt not take the name of the LORD thy God in vain: the LORD will not hold him guiltless that taketh his name in vain.[Exd.20:4-7 KJV]. But we have his treasure in earthen vessels, that the excellency of the power may be od God, and not of us. We are troubled on every side, yet not distressed; we are perplexed, but not in despair; Persecuted, but not forsaken; cast down, but not destroyed; Always bearing about in the body the dying of the Lord Jesus, that the life also of Jesus might be manifest in our body. For we which live are alway delivered unto death for Jesus' sake, that the life also of Jesus might be made manifest in our mortal flesh.[2 Cor.4:7-11 KJV].

REFLECTION:

_____

_____

_____

_____

_____

_____

_____

_____

_____

_____

_____

_____

_____

_____

_____

_____

_____

_____

_____

_____

_____

_____

Knowing that He which raised up the Lord Jesus shall raise up us also by Jesus, and shall present us with you. For all things are for your sakes, that the abundant grace might through the thanksgiving of many redound to the glory of God. For which cause we faint not: but though our outward man perish, yet the inward man is renewed day by day. For our light affliction, which is but for a moment, worketh for us a far more exceeding and eternal weight of glory; While we look not at the things which are seen, but at the things which are not seen: for the things which are seen are temporal; but the things which are not seen are eternal.[2 Cor.4:14-18 KJV]. The mind is an intangible part of the human soul: the mind has the ability to control the human spirit and body, Wherever the mind goes, the body follows: oir mindset can either free us or keep us in bondage. A mind that stays with God is a mind that meditates on the Word of God day and night. Such a person will enjoy peace and prosperity. Blessed is the man that walketh not in the counsel of the ungodly, nor standeth in the way of sinners, nor sitteth in the seat of the scornful. But his delight is in the law of the LORD; and in his law doth he meditate day and night. And shall be like a tree planted by the rivers of water, that bringeth forth his fruit in his season; his leaf also shall not wither; and whatsoever he doeth shall prosper. The ungodly are not so: but are like the chaff which the wind driveth away.

Therefore the ungodly shall not stand in the judgment, nor sinners in the congregation of the righteous. For the LORD knoweth the way of the righteous: but the way of the ungodly shall perish[Psalm 1:1-6 KJV]. And be not conformed to this world: but be ye transformed by the renewing of your mind, that ye may prove what is that good, and acceptable, and perfect, will of God[Rom.12:2 KJV]. According to my earnest expectation and my hope, that in nothing I shall be ashamed, but that with all boldness, as always, so now also Christ shall be magnified in my body, whether it be by life, or by death. For to me to live is Christ, and to die is gain.[Phi.1:20,21 KJV]. Who being the brightness of his glory, and the express image of his person, and upholding all things by the word of his power, when he had by himself purged our sins, sat down on the right hand of the Majesty on high; Being made so much better than the angels, as he hath by inheritance obtained a more excellent name than they. For unto which of the angels said he at any time, Thou art my Son, thisday have I begotten thee? And again, I will be to him a Father, and he shall be to me a Son? And again, when he bringeth in the firstbegotten into the world, he saith, And let all the angels of God worship him. But unto the Son he saith, Thy throne, O God, is for ever and ever: a sceptre of thy kingdom. And, Thou, Lord, in the beginning hast laid the foundation of the earth; and the heavens are the works of thine hands.[Heb.1:3-6,8,10 KJV]. An fear not them which kill the body, but not able to kill the soul: but rather fear him which is able to destroy both soul and body in hell.[Mat.10:28 KJV]. Knowing this, that the trying of your faith worketh patience. But let patience have her perfect work, that ye may be perfect and entire, wanting nothing. If any of you lack wisdom, let him ask of God, that giveth to all men liberally, and upbraideth not; and it shall be given him.[James 1:3-5 KJV].

REFLECTION:

_____

_____

_____

_____

_____

_____

_____

_____

_____

_____

_____

_____

_____

_____

_____

_____

_____

_____

_____

_____

_____

_____

For whatsoever is born of God overcometh the world: and this is the victory that overcometh the world, even our faith. Who is he that overcometh the world, but he that believeth that Jesus is the Son of God? This is he that came by water and blood, even Jesus Christ; not by water only, but by water and blood. And it is the Spirit that beareth witness, because the Spirit is truth. For there are three that bear record in heaven, the Father, the Word, and the Holy Ghost: and these three are one. And there are three that bear witness in earth, the Spirit, and the water, and the blood: and these three agree in one. These things have I written unto you that believe on the name of the Son of God; that ye may know that ye have eternal life, and that ye may believe on the name of the Son of God. And this is the confidence that we have in him, that, if we ask any thing according to his will, he heareth us: And if we know that he hear us, whatsoever we ask, we know that we have the petitions that we desired of him. And we know that we are of God, and the whole world lieth in wickedness. And we know that the Son of God is come, and hath given us an understanding, that we may know him that is true, and we are in him that is true, even his Son Jesus Christ. This is the true God, and eternal life. [1 John 5:4-8,13-15,19,20 KJV]. The LORD will give strength unto his people; the LORD will bless his people with peace.[29:11 KJV]. He hath made every thing beautiful in his time: he hath set the world in their heart, so that no man can find out the work that God maketh from the beginning to the end. I know that there is no good in them, but for a man to rejoice, and to do good in his life. And also that every man should eat and drink, and enjoy the good of all his labour, it is the gift of God. I know that, whatsoever God doeth, it shall be for ever: nothing can be put to it, nor any thing taken from it: and God doeth it, that men should fear before him. That which hath been is now; and that which is to be hath already been; and God requireth that which is past.[Ecc.3:11-15 KJV]. For even Christ pleased not himself; but, as it is written, The reproaches of them that reproached thee fell on me. For whatsoever things were written aforetime were written for our learning, that we through patience and comfort of the scriptures might have hope. Now the God of patience and consolation grant you to be likeminded one toward another according to Christ Jesus: That ye may with one mind and one mouth glorify God, even the Father of our Lord Jesus Christ. Wherefore receive ye one another, as Christ also received us to the glory of God,[Rom.15:3-7 KJV]. The moment you become born again, you are born into a heavenly family, The heavenly family has one purpose and that purpose is to please God, The eternal life given to a believer in Christ Jesus is to live for Christ while on this earth. Leading people to Christ is the believer's number one purpose and, as the apostle Paul said, ro die for the gospel is to gain because you are going to heaven to be with Jesus forever.

REFLECTION:

_____

_____

_____

_____

_____

_____

_____

_____

_____

_____

_____

_____

_____

_____

_____

_____

_____

_____

_____

_____

_____

What? Know ye not that your body is the temple of the Holy Ghost which is in you, which ye have of God, and ye are not your own? For ye are bought with a price: therefore glorify God in your body, and in your spirit, which are God.s.[1 Cor.6:19,20 KJV]. For if a man think himself to be something, when he is nothing, he deceiveth himself. But let every man prove his own work, and then shall he have rejoicing in himself alone and not in another. For every man shall bear his own burden. Let him that is taught in the word communicate unto him that teacheth in all good things. Be not deceived; God is not mocked: for whatsoever a man soweth, that shall he also reap. For he that soweth to his flesh shall of the flesh reap corruption; but he that soweth to the Spirit shall of the Spirit reap life everlasting. From henceforth let no man trouble me: for I bear in my body the marks of the Lord Jesus. [Gal.6:3-8,17 KJV]. And walk in love, as Christ also hath loved us, and hath given himself for us an offering and a sacrifice to god for a sweetsmelling savour. But fornication, and all uncleanness, or covetousness, let it not be once named among you, as becometh saints; Neither filthiness, nor foolish talking, nor jesting, which are not convenient: but rather giving of thanks. For this ye know, that no whoremonger, nor unclean person, nor covetous man, who is an idolater, hath any inheritance in the kingdom of Christ and of God. Let no man deceive you with vain words: for because of these things cometh the wrath of God upon the children of disobedience. Be not ye therefore partakers with them. For ye were sometimes darkness, but now are ye light in the Lord: walk as children of light: (For the fruit of the Spirit is in all goodness and righteousness and truth;) Proving what is acceptable unto the Lord. And have no fellowship with the unfruitful works of darkness, but rather reprove them. For it is a shame even to speak of those things which are done of them in secret. But all things that are reproved are made manifest by the light: for whatsoever doth make manifest is light. Wherefore he saith, Awake thou that sleepest, and arise from the dead, and Christ shall give thee light. See then that ye walk circumspectly, not as fools, but as wise, Redeeming the time because the days are evil. Wherefore be ye not unwise, but understanding what the will of the Lord is. And be not drunk with wine, wherein is excess; but be filled with the Spirit; Giving thanks always for all things unto God and the Father in the name of our Lord Jesus Christ; Submitting yourselves one to another in the fear of God.[Eph.5:2-18,20,21 KJV]. Blessed is the man that trusteth in the LORD, and whose hope the :LORD is. For he shall be as a tree planted by the waters, and that spreadeth out her roots by the river, and shall not see when heat cometh, but her leaf shall be green; and shall not be careful in the year of drought, neither shall cease from yielding fruit. The heart is deceitful above all things, and desperately wicked: who can know it? I the LORD search the heart, I try the reins, even to give every man according to his ways, and according to the fruit of his doings. Heal me, O LORD, and I shall be healed; save me, and I shall be saved: for thou art my praise. Behold, they say unto me, Where is the word of the LORD? Let it come now.[Jer.17:7-10,14,15 KJV].

REFLECTION:

_____

_____

_____

_____

_____

_____

_____

_____

_____

_____

_____

_____

_____

_____

_____

_____

_____

_____

_____

_____

_____

_____

There is no power in the heavens and on earth and under the earth; is more powerful than the power of God: for God is power. There is no strength in the heavens and earth and under the earth; is stronger than God: for God is strength. God is love: God is the shield and buckler to those of us who put all of our trust in Him. Known unto God are all his works from the beginning of the world,[Acts 15:18 KJV]. For great is the LORD, and greatly to be praised: he also is to be feared above all gods. For all the gods of the people are idols: but the LORD made the heavens. Glory and honour are in his presence; strength and gladness are in his place. Give unto the LORD, ye kindreds of the people, give unto the LORD glory and strength. Give unto the LORD the glory due unto his name: bring an offering, and come before him: worship the LORD in the beauty of holiness. Fear before him, all the earth: the world also shall be stable, that be not moved. Let the heavens be glad, and let the earth rejoice: and let men say among the nations, The LORD reigneth. Let the sea roar, and the fulness thereof: let the fields rejoice, and all that is therein. Then shall the trees of the wood sing out at the presence of the LORD, because he cometh to judge the earth. O give thanks unto the LORD; for he is good; for his mercy endureth for ever.[1 Chr. 16:25-34 KJV]. Lord hear my voice: let thine ears be attentive to the voice of my supplications.

If thou, LORD, shouldest mark iniquities, O Lord, who shall stand? But there is forgiveness with thee, that thou mayest be feared. I wait for the LORD, my soul doth wait, and in his word do I hope. My soul waiteth for the Lord more than they that watch for the morning: I say, more than they that watch for the morning. [Psalm.130:2-6 KJV]. LORD, my heart is not haughty, nor mine eyes lofty: neither do I exercise myself in great matters, or in things too high for me. Surely I have behaved and quieted myself, as a child that is weaned of his mother: my soul is even as a weaned child.[Psalm.131:1-3 KJV]. Give ear to my words, O LORD, consider my meditation. Hearken unto the voice of my cry, my King, and my God: for unto thee will I pray. My voice shalt thou hear in the morning, O LORD; in the morning will I direct my prayer unto thee, and will look up. For thou art not a Dod that hath pleasure in wickedness: neither shall evil dwell with thee.Let all those that put their trust in thee rejoice: let them ever shout for joy, because thou defendest them: let them also that love thy name be joyful in thee. For thou, LORD wilt bless the righteous; with favour wilt thou compass him as with a shield.[Psalm 5:1-4,11,12 KJV]. I am the man that hath seen affliction by the rod of his wrath. He hath hedged ne about, that I cannot get out: he hath made my chain heavy. Also when I cry and shout, he shutterh out my prayer. He hath inclosed my ways with hewn stone, he hath made my paths crooked. He hath turned aside my ways, and pulled me in pieces: he hath made me desolate. He hath bent his bow, and set me as a mark for the arrow. He hath caused the arrows of his quiver to enter into my reins. My soul hath them still in remembrance, and is humbled in me. This I recall to my mind, therefore have I hope. It is of the LORD's mercies that we are not consumed, because his compassions fail not.They are new every morning: great is thy faithfulness. The LORD is my portion, saith my soul; therefore will I hope in him. The LORD is good unto them that wait for him, to the soul that seeketh him. It is good that a man should both hope and quietly wait for the salvation of the LORD.[Lam.3:1,7-9,11-13-26 KJV].

REFLECTION:

_____

_____

_____

_____

_____

_____

_____

_____

_____

_____

_____

_____

_____

_____

_____

_____

_____

_____

_____

_____

And now, O Father, glorify thou me with thine own self with the glory which I had with thee before the world was. I have manifested thy name unto the men which thou gavest me out of the world: thine they were, and thou gavest them me: and they kept thy word. Now they have known that all things whatsoever thou hast given me are of thee. For I have given unto them the words which thou gavest me; and they have received them, and have known surely that I came out of thee, and they have believed that thou didst send me. I pray for them: I pray not for the world, but for them which thou hast given me; for they are thine. And all mine are thine, and thine are mine; and I am glorified in them. And now I am no more in the world, but these are in the world, and I come to thee. Holy Father, I keep through thine own name those whom thou hast given me, that they may be one as we are.[John 17:5-11 KJV]. For they being ignorant of God's righteousness and going about to establish their own righteousness, have not submitted themselves unto the righteous of God. For Christ is the end of the law for righteousness to every one that believeth. But the righteousness which is of faith speaketh on this wise, Say not in thine heart, Who shall ascend into heaven? (that is, to bring up Christ again from the dead.) But what saith it? The word is nigh thee, even in thy mouth, and thy heart: that is, the word of faith, which we preach; That if thou confess with thy mouth the Lord Jesus, and shalt believe in thine heart that God hath raised him from the dead, thou shalt be saved. For with the heart man believeth unto righteousness; and with the mouth confession is made unto salvation. For whosoever shall call upon the name of the Lord shall be saved. So then faith cometh by hearing, and hearing by the word of God. [Rom.10:3,4,6-10,13,17 KJV]. That ye may be mindful of the words which were spoken before by the holy prophets, and of the commandment of the apostles of the Lord and Savour: Knowing this first, that there shall come in the last days scoffers, walking after their own lusts, And saying, Where is the promise of his coming? For since the fathers fell asleep, all things continue as they were from the beginning of the creation. For this they willingly are ignorant of, that by the word of God the heavens were of old, and the earth standing out of the water and in the water: Whereby the world that then was, being overflowed with water, perished: But the heavens and the earth, which are now, by the same word are kept in store, reserved unto fire against the day of judgment and perdition of ungodly men. But, beloved, be not ignorant of this one thing, that one day is with the Lord as a thousand years, and a thousand years as one day. But the day of the Lord will come as a thief in the night; in which the heavens shall pass away with a great noise, and the elements shall melt with fervent heat, the earth also and the works that are therein shall be burned up. Seeing then that all these things shall be dissolved, what manner of persons ought ye to be in all holy conversation and godliness, Looking for and hasting unto the coming of the day of God, wherein the heavens being on fire shall be dissolved, and the elements shall melt with fervent heat? Nevertheless we, according to his promise, look for new heavens and a new earth, wherein dwelleth righteousness. Wherefore, beloved, seeing that ye look for such things, be diligent that ye may be found of him in peace, without spot, and blameless. But grow in grace, and in the knowledge of our Lord and Savior Jesus Christ. To him be glory both now and for ever. Amen. [2Pet.3:2-14,18 KJV].

REFLECTION:

_____

_____

_____

_____

_____

_____

_____

_____

_____

_____

_____

_____

_____

_____

_____

_____

_____

_____

_____

_____

_____

_____

_____

Abide in me, and I in you. As the branch cannot bear fruit of itself, except it abide in the vine; no more can ye, except ye abide in me. I am the vine, ye are the branches: He that abideth in me, and I in him, the same bringeth forth much fruit: for without me ye can do nothing, If a man abide not in me, he is cast forth as a branch, and is withered; and men gather them, and cast them into the fire, and they are burned. If ye abide in me, and my words abide in you, ye shall ask what ye will, and it shall be done unto you. Herein is my Father glorified, that ye bear much fruit; so shall ye be my disciples. As the Father hath loved me, so have I loved you: continue ye in my love.If ye keep my commandments, ye shall abide in my love; even as I have kept my Father's commandments, and abide in his love. Ye have not chosen me, but I have chosen you, and ordained you, that ye should go and bring forth fruit, and that your fruit should remain: that whatsoever ye shall ask of the Father in my name, he may give it you. These things I command you, that ye love one another. If the world hate you, ye know that it hated me before it hated you. If ye were of the world, the world would love his own: but because ye are not of the world, but I have chosen you out of the world, therefore the world hateth you. But this cometh to pass, that the word might be fulfilled that is written in their law, They hated me without a cause. But when the Comforter is come, whom I will send unto you from the Father, even the Spirit of truth, which proceedeth from the Father, he shall testify of me.[John 15:4-10.16-19,26 KJV]. Be strong in the Lord, and in the power of his might. Put on the whole armour of God, that ye may be able to stand against the wiles of the devil. For we wrestle not against flesh and blood, but against principalities, against powers, against the rulers of the darkness of this world, against spiritual wickedness in high places. Stand therefore, having your loins girt about with truth, and having on the breastplate of righteousness; And your feet shod with the preparation of the gospel of peace; Above all, taking the shield of faith, wherewith ye shall be able to quench all the fiery darts of the wicked. And take the helmet of salvation, and the sword of the Spirit, which is the word of God: Praying always with all prayer and supplication in the Spirit, and watching thereunto with all perseverance and supplication for the saints.[Eph.6:10-12,14-18 KJV]. Put them in mind to be subject to principalities and powers, to obey magistrates, to be ready to every good work. To speak evil of no man, to be no brawlers, but gentle, shewing all meekness unto all men. For we ourselves also were sometimes foolish, disobedient, deceived, serving divers lusts and pleasures, living in malice and envy, hateful, hating one another. But after that the kindness and love of God our Saviour toward man appeared, Not by works of righteousness which we have done, but according to his mercy he saved us, by the washing of regeneration, and renewing of the Holy Ghost; Which he shed on us abundantly through Jeaua Christ our Saviour; that being justified by his grace, we should be made heirs according to the hope of eternal life.[Titus 3:1-7

REFLECTION:

_____

_____

_____

_____

_____

_____

_____

_____

_____

_____

_____

_____

_____

_____

_____

_____

_____

_____

_____

_____

_____

_____

All things are delivered unto me of my Father; and no man knoweth the Son, but the Father, save the Son, and he to whomsoever the Son will reveal him. Come unto me, all ye that labour and are heavy laden, and I will give you rest. Take my yoke upon you, and learn of me; for I am meek and lowly in heart: and ye shall find rest unto your souls. For my yoke is easy, and my burden is light.[Mat.11:27-30 KJV]. But I say unto you which hear, Love your enemies, do good to them which hate you. Judge not, and ye shall not be judged: condemn not, and ye shall not be condemned: forgive, and ye shall be forgiven.[Luke 6:27,37 KJV]. Now the God of hope fill you with all joy and peace in believing, that ye may abound in hope through the power of the Holy Ghost. [Rom.15:13 KJV]. And I will give unto thee the keys of the kingdom of heaven: and whatsoever thou shalt bind on earth shall be bound in heaven: and whatsoever thou shalt loose on earth shall be loosed in heaven. If any man will come after me, let him deny himself, and take up his cross, and follow me. For whosoever will save his life shall lose it: and whosoever will lose his life for my sake shall find it. For what is a man profited, if he shall gain the whole world, and lose his own soul? Or what shall a man give in exchange for his soul? For the Son of man shall come in the glory of his Father with his angels; and then he shall reward every man according to his works.

[Mat.16:19,24-27 KJV]. For there is nothing covered, that shall not be revealed; neither hid, that shall not be known. Therefore whatsoever ye have spoken in darkness shall be heard in the light; and that which ye have spoken in the ear in closets shall be proclaimed upon the housetops. And I say unto you my friends, Be not afraid of them that kill the body, and after that have no more that they can do. But I will forewarn you whom ye shall fear: Fear him, which after he hath killed hath power to cast into hell; yea I say unto you, Fear him. And seek not ye what ye shall eat, or what ye shall drink, neither be ye of doubtful mind. For all these things do the nations of the world seek after: and your Father knoweth that ye have need of these things. But rather seek ye the kingdom of God; and all these things shall be added unto you. Fear not, little flock; for it is your Father's good pleasure to give you the kingdom.[Luke 12:2-5,29-32 KJV]. Have faith in God. For verily I say unto you, That whosoever shall say unto this mountain, Be thou removed, and be thou cast into the sea; and shall not doubt in his heart, but shall believe that those things which he saith shall come to pass; he shall have whatsoever he saith. Therefore I say unto you, What things soever ye desire, when ye pray, believe that ye receive them, and ye shall have them. And when ye stand praying, forgive, if ye have ought against any: that your Father also which is in heaven may forgive you your trespasses. But if ye do not forgive, neither will your Father which is in heaven forgive your trespasses.[Mark 11:22-26 KJV]. Jesus knowing that the Father had given all things into his hands, and that he was come from God, and went to God. Peter saith unto him, Thou shalt never wash my feet. Jesus answered him, If I wash thee not, thou hast no part with me. Jesus saith to him, He that is washed needeth not save to wash his feet, but is clean every whit: ye are clean. Verily, verily, I say unto you. The servant is not greater than his lord; neither he that is sent greater than he that sent him. A new commandment I give unto you, That ye love one another; as I have loved you, that ye also love one another.[John 13:3,8,10,16,34 KJV].

REFLECTION:

_____

_____

_____

_____

_____

_____

_____

_____

_____

_____

_____

_____

_____

_____

_____

_____

_____

_____

_____

_____

_____

_____

Behold, what manner of love the Father hath bestowed upon us, that we should be called the sons of God: therefore the world knoweth us not. Beloved, now are we the sons of God and it doth not yet appear what we shall be: but we know that, when he shall appear, we shall be like him; for we shall see him as he is. And every man that hath this hope in him purifieth himself, even as he is pure. Whosoever committeth sin transgresseth also the law: for sin is the transgression of the law. And ye know that he was manifested to take away our sins; and in him is no sin. Whosoever abideth in him sinneth not: whosoever sinneth hath not seen him, neither known him. Little children, let no man deceive you: he that doeth righteousness is righteous, even as he is righteous. He that committeth sin is of the devil; for the devil sinneth from the beginning, For this purpose the Son of God was manifested, that he might destroy the works of the devil. Whosoever is born of God doth not commit sin; for his seed remaineth in him: and he cannot sin, because he is born of God. In this the children of God are manifest, and the children of the devil: whosoever doeth not righteousness is not of God, neither he loveth not his brother. For this is the message that ye heard from the beginning, that we should love one another. My little children, let us not love in word, neither in tongue; but in deed and in truth. And hereby we know that we are of the truth, and shall assure our hearts before him. For if our heart condemn us, God is greater than our heart, and knoweth all things. Beloved, if our heart condemn us not, then have we confidence toward God. And whatsoever we ask, we receive of him, because we keep his commandments, and do those things that are pleasing in his sight. And this is his commandment, That we should believe on the name of his Son Jesus Christ, and love one another, as he gave us commandment. And he that keepeth his commandments dwelleth in him, and he in him. And hereby we know that he abideth in us, by the Spirit which he hath given us.[1 John 3:1-11,18-24 KJV]. The preparation of the heart of msan, and the answer of the tongue, is from the LORD. All the ways of a man are clean in his own eyes; but the LORD weigheth the spirits. Commit thy works unto the LORD, and thy thoughts shall be established. The LORD hath made all things for himself: yea, even the wicked for the day of evil. Every one that is proud in heart is an abomination to the LORD: though hand join hand, he shall not be unpunished. By mercy and truth iniquity is purged: and by the fear of the LORD men depart from evil. When a man's ways please the LORD, he maketh even his enemies to be at peace with him. **Better is a little with righteousness than great revenues without right. A man's heart deviseth his way; but the LORD directeth his steps.[Prov.16:1-9 KJV]. How much better is it to get wisdom than** gold! And to get understanding rather than silver! The highway of the upright is to depart from evil: he that keepeth his way preserveth his soul. Pride goeth before destruction, and an haughty spirit before fall. Better it is to be of an humble spirit with the lowly, than to divide the spoil with the proud. He that handleth a matter wisely shall find good: and whoso trusteth in the LORD, happy is he. The wise in heart shall be called prudent: and the sweetness of his lips increaseth learning. Understanding is a wellspring of life unto him that hath it: but the instruction of fools is folly. The heart of the wise teacheth his mouth, and addeth learning to his lips. PLeasant words are as an honeycomb,sweet to the soul, and heath to the bones. There is a way that seemeth right unto man, but the end thereof are the ways of death. He that laboureth laboureth for himself; for his mouth craveth it of him. An ungodly man diggeth up evil: and his lips there is a burning fire.[Prov.16:16-27 KJV].

REFLECTION:

_____

_____

_____

_____

_____

_____

_____

_____

_____

_____

_____

_____

_____

_____

_____

_____

_____

_____

_____

_____

There is therefore now no condemnation to them which are in Christ Jesus, who walk not after the flesh, but after the Spirit. For the law of the Spirit of life in Christ Jesus hath made me free from the law of sin and death. For what the law could not do, in that it was weak through flesh, God sending his own Son in the likeness of sinful flesh, and for sin, condemned sin in the flesh. That the righteousness of the law might be fulfilled in us, who walk not after the flesh, but after the Spirit. For they that are after the flesh do mind the things of the flesh; but they that are after the Spirit the things of the Spirit. For to be carnally minded is death; but to be spiritually minded is life and peace. Because the carnal mind is enmity against God: for it is not subject to the law of God, neither indeed can be. So then they that are in the flesh cannot please God. [Rom.8:1-8 KJV]. That their hearts might be comforted, being knit together in love, and unto all riches of the full assurance of understanding,to the acknowledgement of the mystery of God, and of the father, and of Christ; In whom are hid all the treasures of wisdom and knowledge. And this I say, lest any man should beguile you with enticing words. For though I be absent in the flesh, yet am I with you in spirit, joying and beholding your order, and the stedfastness of your faith in Christ. As ye have therefore received Christ Jesus Lord, so walk ye in him: Rooted and built up in him, and stablished in faith, as ye have been taught, abounding therein with thanksgiving. Beware lest any man spoil you through philosophy and vain deceit, after the tradition of men, after the rudiments of the world, and not after Christ. For in him dwelleth all the fulness of the Godhead bodily. And ye are complete in him, which is the head of all principality and power: In whom also ye are circumcised with the circumcision made without hands, in putting off the body of the sins of the flesh by the circumcision of Christ: Buried with him in baptism, wherein also ye are risen with him through the faith of the operation of God, who hath raised him from the dead. And you, being dead in your sins and the circumcision of your flesh, hath he quickened together with him, having forgiven you all trespasses; Blotting out the handwriting of ordinances that was against us, which was contrary to us, and took it out of the way, nailing it to his cross; And having spoiled principalities and powers, he made shew of them openly, triumphing over them in it.[Col.2:2-15 KJV]. Hear me when I call. O God of my righteousness: thou hast enlarged me when I was in distress; have mercy upon me, and hear my prayer. But know that the LORD hath set apart him that is godly for himself: the LORD will hear when I call unto him.[Psalm 4:1,3 KJV]. Forasmuch then as we are the offspring of God, we ought not to think that the Godhead is like unto gold, or silver, or stone, graven by art and man's device.

And the times of this ignorance God winked at; but now commandeth all men every where to repent: Because he hath appointed a day, in the which he will judge the world in righteousness by that man whom he hath ordained; whereof he given assurance unto all men, in that he hath raised him from the dead.[Acts 17:29-31 KJV].

REFLECTION:

For it is God which worketh in you both to will and to do of his good pleasure. Do all things without murmurings and disputings: That ye may be blameless and harmless, the sons of god, without rebuke, in the midst of a crooked and perverse nation, among whom ye shine as lights in the world; Holding forth the word of life; that I may rejoice in the day of Christ, that I have not run in vain, neither laboured in vain.[Phli.2:13-16 KJV]. For in many things we offend all. If any man offend not in word, the same is a perfect man, and able also to bridle the whole body. Behold also the ships, which though they be so great, and are driven of fierce winds, yet are they turned about with a very small helm, whithersoever the governor listeth. Even so the tongue is a little member, and boasteth great things. Behold, how a great a matter a little fire kindleth! And the tongue is a fire, a world of iniquity: so is the tongue among our members, that it defileth the whole body, and setteth on fire the course of nature; and it is set on fire of hell. For every kind of beasts, and of birds, and of serpents, and of things in the sea, is tamed, and hath been tamed of mankind: But the tongue can no man tame; it is an unruly evil, full of deadly poison. Therewith bless we God, even the Father; and therewith curse we men, which are made after the similitude of God. Out of the same mouth proceedeth blessing and cursing, My brethren, these things ought not so to be. For where envying and strife is, there is confusion and every evil work. But the wisdom that is from above is first pure, then peaceable, gentle, and easy to be entreated, full of mercy and good fruits, without partiality, and without hypocrisy. And the fruit of righteousness is sown in peace of them that make peace.[Jam.3:2-10,16-18 KJV]. For the law having a shadow of good things to come, and not the very image of the things, can never with those sacrifices which they offered year by year continually make the comers thereunto perfect. For then would they not have ceased to be offered? Because that the worshippers once purged should have had no more conscience of sins. But in those sacrifices there is a remembrance again made of sins every year. For it is not possible that the blood of bulls and of goats should take away sins. Wherefore when he cometh into the world, he saith, Sacrifice and offering thou wouldest not, but a body hast thou prepared me. In burnt offerings and sacrifices for sin thou hast had no pleasure. Then said I, Lo, I come (in the volume of the book it is written of me,) to do thy will, O God. Then said he, Lo, I come to do thy will, O God, He taketh away the first, that he may establish the second. By the which will we are sanctified through the offering of the body of Jesus Christ once for all. But this man, after he had offered one sacrifice for sins for ever, sat down on the right hand of God; From henceforth expecting till his enemies be made his footstool. For by one offering he hath perfected for ever them that are sanctified. Whereof the Holy Ghost also is a witness to us: after that he had said before, This is the covenant that I will make with them after those days, saith the Lord, I will put my laws into their hearts, and in their minds will I write them; And their sins and iniquities will I remember no more. Now where remission of these is, there is no more offering for sin. Having therefore, brethren, boldness to enter into the holiest by the blood of Jesus.[Heb.10:1-7,9,10,12-19 KJV].

REFLECTION:

_____

_____

_____

_____

_____

_____

_____

_____

_____

_____

_____

_____

_____

_____

_____

_____

_____

_____

_____

_____

_____

_____

For I am the LORD, I change not; Even from the days of your fathers ye are gone away from mine ordinances, and have not kept them. Return unto me, and I will return unto you, saith the LORD of hosts. But ye said, Wherein shall we return?[Malachi 3:6,7 KJV]. Preserve me, O God: for in thee do I put my trust. O my soul, thou hast said unto the LORD, Thou art my Lord: my goodness extendeth not to thee; I will bless the LORD, who hath given me counsel: my reins also instruct me in the night seasons. I have set the LORD always before me: because he is at my right hand, I shall not be moved. Therefore my heart is glad, and my glory rejoiceth: my flesh also shall rest in hope. For thou wilt not leave my soul in hell; neither wilt thou suffer thine Holy One to see corruption. Thou wilt shew me the path of life: in thy presence is fulness of joy; at thy right hand here are pleasures for evermore.[Psalm 16:1,2,7-11 KJV]. Delight thyself also in the LORD; and he shall give thee the desires of thine heart. Commit thy way unto the LORD; trust also in him; and he shall bring it to pass. And he shall bring forth thy righteousness as the light, and thy judgment as the noonday. Rest in the LORD, and wait patiently for him: fret not thyself because of him who prospereth in his way, because of the man who bringeth wicked devices to pass. Cease from anger, and forsake wrath: fret not thyself wise to do evil. For evildoers shall be cut off: but those that wait upon the LORD, they shall inherit the earth.[Psalm 37:4-9 KJV]. Doth not behave itself unseemly, seeketh not her own, is not easily provoked, thinketh no evil; Rejoiceth not in iniquity, but rejoiceth in the truth; Beareth all things, believeth all things, hopeth all things, endureth all things. Charity never faileth: but whether there be prophecies, they shall fail; whether there be tongues, they shall cease; whether there be knowledge, it shall vanish away. But when that which is perfect is come, then that which is in part shall be done away. When I was a child, I spake as a child, I understood as a child, I thought as a child: but when I became a man, I put away childish things. For now we see through a glass, darkjy; but then face to face: now I know in part; but then shall I know even as also I am known. And now abideth faith, hope, charity, these three; but the greatest of these is charity.[1 Cor.13:5-8,10-13 KJV]. For I reckon that the sufferings of this present time are not worthy to be compared with the glory which shall be revealed in us. For the earnest expectation of the creature waiteth for the manifestation of the sons of God. For we know that the whole creation groaneth and travaileth in pain together until now. And not only they, but ourselves also, which have the firstfruits of the Spirit, even we ourselves groan within ourselves, waiting for the adoption, to wit, the redemption of our body. For we are saved by hope: but hope that is seen is not hope: for what a man seeth, why doth he yet hope for? But if we hope for that we see not, then do we with patience wait for it.[Rom.8:18,19,22-25 KJV]. Whereby are given unto us exceeding great and precious promises: that by these ye might be partakers of the divine nature, having escaped the corruption that is in the world through lust. Amd beside this, giving all diligence, add to your faith virtue; and to virtue knowledge: And to knowledge temperance; and to temperance patience; and to patience godliness; And to godliness brotherly kindness; and to brotherly kindness charity. For if these things be in you, and abound, they make you that ye shall neither be barren nor unfruitful in the knowledge of our Lord Jesus Christ. [2 Peter 1:4-8 KJV].

REFLECTION:

_____
_____
_____
_____
_____
_____
_____
_____
_____
_____
_____
_____
_____
_____
_____
_____
_____
_____
_____
_____
_____
_____

For many shall come in my name, saying, I am Christ; and shall deceive many. And when ye shall hear of wars and rumours of wars, be ye not troubled: for such things must needs be; but the end shall not be yet. For nation shall rise against nation, and kingdom against kingdom: and there shall be earthquakes in divers places, and there shall be famines and troubles: these are the beginnings of sorrows. For in those days shall be affliction, such as was not from the beginning of the creation which God created unto this time, neither shall be. And except that the Lord had shortened those days, no flesh should be saved: but for the elect's sake, whom he hath chosen, he hath shortened the days. And then if any man shall say to you, Lo, here is Christ; or, lo he is there; believe him not: For false Christs and false prophets shall rise, and shall shew signs and wonders, to seduce, if it were possible, even the elect. But take ye heed: hehold, I have foretold you all things. But in those days, after that tribulation, the sun shall be darkened, and the moon shall not give her light, And the stars of heaven shall fall, and the powers that are in heaven shall be shaken. And then shall they see the Son of man coming in the clouds with great power and glory. And then shall he send his angels, and shall gather together his elect from the four winds, from the uttermost part of the earth to the uttermost part of heaven. Heaven and earth shall pass away: but my words shall not pass away.

But of that day and that hour knoweth no man, no, not the angels which are in heaven, neither the Son, but the Father.[Mark 13:6-8,19-27,31,32 KJV]. Put on therefore, as the elect of God, holy and beloved, bowels of mercies, kindness, humbleness of mind, meekness, longsuffering; Forbearing one another, and forgiving one another, if any man have a quarrel against any: even as Christ forgave you, so also do ye. And above all these things put on charity, which is the bond of perfectness. And let the peace of God rule in your hearts, to the which also ye are called in one body; and be thankful. Let the word of Christ dwell in you richly in all wisdom; teaching and admonishing one another in psalms and hymns and spiritual songs, singing with grace in your hearts to the Lord. And whatsoever ye do in word or deed, do all in the name of the Lord Jesus, giving thanks to God and the Father by him.[Col.3:12-17 KJV]. From whence come wars and fightings among you? Come they not hence, even of your lusts that war in your members? Ye list, and have not: ye kill, and desire to have, and cannot obtain: ye fight and war, yet ye have not, because ye ask not. Ye ask, and receive not, because ye ask amiss, that ye may consume it upon your lusts. Ye adulterers and adulteresses, know ye not that the friendship of the world is enmity with God? Whosoever therefore will be a friend of the world is the enemy of God. Do ye think that the scripture saith in vain, The spirit that dwelleth in us lusteth to envy? But he giveth more grace. Wherefore he saith, God resisteth the proud, but giveth grace unto the humble. Draw nigh to God, and he will draw nigh to you. Cleanse your hands, ye sinners; and purify your hearts, ye double minded. Submit yourselves therefore to God. Resist the devil, and he will flee from you.[James 4:1-8 KJV].

REFLECTION:

_____
_____
_____
_____
_____
_____
_____
_____
_____
_____
_____
_____
_____
_____
_____
_____
_____
_____
_____
_____
_____
_____

At the beginning of thy supplications the commandment came forth, and I am come to shew thee; for thou art greatly beloved: therefore understand the matter, and consider the vision. Seventy weeks are determined upon thy people and upon thy holy city, to finish the transgression, and to make an end of sins, and to make reconciliation for iniquity, and to bring in everlasting righteousness, and to seal up the vision and prophecy, and to anoint the most Holy.[Dan.9:23,24 KJV]. Who comforteth us in all our tribulation, that we may be able to comfort them which are in any trouble, by the comfort wherewith we ourselves are comforted of God. For as the sufferings of Christ abound in us, so our consolation also aboundeth by Christ.[2 Cor.1:4,5 KJV]. If there be therefore any consolation in Christ, if any comfort of love, if any fellowship of the Spirit, if any bowels and mercies, Fulfil ye my joy, that ye be likeminded, having the same love, being of one accord, of one mind. Let nothing be done through strife or vainglory; but in lowliness of mind let each esteem other better than themselves. For all seek their own, not the things which are Jesus Christ's.[Phi.2:1-3,21 KJV]. Know ye not that the unrighteous shall not inherit the kingdom of God? Be not deceived: neither fornicators, nor idolaters, nor adulterers, nor effeminate, nor abusers of themselves with mankind, nor thieves, nor covetous, nor drunkards, nor revilers, nor extortioners, shall inherit the kingdom of God. And such were some of you: but ye are washed, but ye are sanctified, but ye are justified in the name of the Lord Jesus, and by the Spirit of our God. All things are lawful unto me, but all things are not expedient: all things are lawful for me, but I will not be brought under the power of any. Meats for the belly, and the belly for the meats, but God shall destroy both it and them. Now the body is not for fornication, but for the Lord; and the Lord for the body. And God hath both raised up the Lord, and will also raise up us by his own power. Know ye not that your bodies are the members of Christ? Shall I then take the members of Christ, and make them the members of an harlot? God forbid. What? Know ye not that he which is joined an harlot is one body? For two, saith he, shall be one flesh. But he that is joined unto the Lord is one spirit.[1 Cor.6:9-17 KJV]. Ye are the light of the world. A city that is set on an hill cannot be hid. Neither do men light a candle, and put it under a bushel, but on a candlestick; and it giveth light unto all that are in the house. Let your light so shine before men, that they may see your good works, and glorify your Father which is in heaven. Think not that I am come to destroy the law, or the prophets: I am not come to destroy, but to fulfil.[Mat.5:14-17 KJV]. He that overcometh shall inherit all things; and I will be his God, and he shall be my son. But the fearful, and unbelieving, and the abominable, and murderers, and whoremongers, and sorcerers, and idolaters, and all liars, shall have their part in the lake which burneth with fire and brimstone: which is the second death.[Rev.21:7,8 KJV].

REFLECTION:

For the Father loveth the Son, and sheweth him all things that himself doeth: and he will shew him greater works than these, that ye may marvel. For the Father raiseth up the dead, and quickeneth them; even so the Son quickeneth whom he will. For the Father judgeth no man, but hath committed all judgment unto the Son: That all men should honour the Son, even as they honour the Father. He that honoureth not the Son honoureth not the Father which hath sent him. Verily, verily, I say unto you, He that heareth my word, and believeth on him that sent me, hath everlasting life, and shall not come into condemnation; but is passed from death unto life. Verily, verily, I say unto you, The hour is coming, and now is, when the dead shall hear the voice of the Son of God: and they that hear shal live. For as the Father hath life in himself; so hath he given to the Son to have life in himself; And hath given him authority to execute judgment also, because he is the Son of mam. Marvel not at this: for the hour is coming, in the which all that are in the graves shall hear his voice, And shall come forth; they that have done good, unto the resurrection of life; and they that have done evil, unto the resurrection of damnation.[John 5:20-29 KJV]. And the Father himself, which hath sent me, hath borne witness of me. Ye have neither heard his voice at any time, nor seen his shape. And ye have not his word abiding in you: for whom he hath sent, him ye believe not. Search the scriptures; for in them ye think ye have eternal life: and they are they which testify of me. And ye will not come to me, that ye might have life.I receive not honour from men. But I know you, that ye have not the love of God in you. I am come in my Father's name, and ye receive me not: if another shall come in his own name, him ye will receive.[John 5:37-43 KJV]. Now we beseech you, brethren, by the coming of our Lord Jesus Christ, and by our gathering together unto him, That ye be not soon shaken in mind, or be troubled, neither by spirit, nor by word, nor by letter as from us, as that the day of Christ is at hand. Let no man deceive you by any means: for that day shall not come, except there come a falling away first, and that man of sin be revealed, the son of perdition; Who opposeth and exalteth above all that is called God, or that is worshipped; so that he as God sitteth in the temple of God, shewing himself that he is God. Remember ye not, that, when I was yet with you, I told you these things? And now ye know what withholdeth that he might be revealed in his time. For the mystery of iniquity doth already work: only he who now letteth will let, until he be taken out of the way. And then shall that Wicked be revealed, whom the Lord shall consume with the spirit of his mouth, and shall destroy with the brightness of his coming: Even him, whose coming is after the working of satan with all power and signs and lying wonders, And with all deceivableness of unrighteousness in them that perish; because they received not the love of the truth, that they might be saved. And for this cause God ahall send them strong delusion, that they should believe a lie: That they all might be damned who believed not the truth, but had pleasure in unrighteousness. But we are bound to give thanks alway to God for you, brethren beloved of the Lord, because God hath from the beginning chosen you to salvation through sanctification of the Spirit and belief of the truth: Whereunto he called you by our gospel, to the obtaining of glory of our Lord Jesus Christ. Therefore, brethren, stand fast, and hold the traditions which ye have been taught, whether by word, or our epistle. Now our Lord Jesus Christ himself, and God, even our Father, which hath loved us, and hath given us everlasting consolation and good hope through grace. Comfort your hearts, and stablish you in every good word and work.[2 Thes.2:2-17 KJV].

REFLECTION:

_____

_____

_____

_____

_____

_____

_____

_____

_____

_____

_____

_____

_____

_____

_____

_____

_____

_____

_____

_____

_____

_____

Finally, brethren, pray for us, that the word of the Lord may have free course, and be glorified, even as it is with you: And that we may be delivered from unreasonable and wicked men: for all men have not faith. But the Lord is faithful, who shall stablish you, and keep you from evil. And we have confidence in the Lord touching you, that ye both do and will do the things which we command you. And the Lord direct your hearts into the love of God, and into patient waiting for Christ. Now them that are such we command and exhort by our Lord Jesus Christ, that with quietness they work, and eat their own bread. But ye brethren, be not weary in well doing. And if any man obey not our word by this epistle, note that man, and have no company with him, that he may be ashamed. Yet count him not as an enemy, but admonish him as a brother. Now the Lord of peace himself give you peace always by all means. The Lord be with you all.[2 Thes.3:1-5,12-16 KJV]. Thou therefore endure hardness, as a good soldier of Jesus Christ. No man that warreth entangleth himself with the affairs of this life; that he may please him who hath chosen him to be a soldier. Wherein I suffer trouble, as an evil doer even unto bonds; but the word of God is not bound. Therefore I endure all things for the elect's sakes, that they may also obtain the salvation which is in Christ Jesus with eternal glory. It is a faithful saying: For if we be dead with him, we shall also live with him. Who concerning the truth have erred, saying that the resurrection is past already; and overthrow the faith of some. Nevertheless the foundation of God standeth sure, having this seal, The Lord knoweth them that are his. And, Let every one that nameth the name of Christ depart from iniquity. Flee also youthful lusts: but follow righteousness, faith, charity, peace, with them that call on the Lord out of a pure heart. And the servant of the Lord must not strive; but be gentle unto all men, apt to teach, patient. In meekness instructing those that oppose themselves; if God peradventure will give them repentance to the acknowledging of the truth; And that they may recover themselves out of the snare of the devil, who are taken captive by him at his will.[2Tim.2:3,4,9-11,18,19,22,24-26 KJV]. When thou passest through the waters, I will be with thee; and through the rivers, they shall not overflow thee: when thou walkest through the fire, thou shalt not be burned; neither shall the flame kindle upon thee. For I am the LORD thy God, the Holy One of Israel, thy Saviour: I gave Egypt for thy ransom, Ethiopia and Seba for thee. Fear not: for I am with thee: I will bring thy seed from the east, and gather those from the west; I will say to the north, Give up; and to the south, Keep not back: bring my sons from far, and my daughters from the ends of the earth; Even every one that is called by my name: for I have created him for my glory, I have formed him; yea, I have made him. I have declared, and have saved, and I have shewed, when there was no strange god among you: therefore ye are witness, saith the LORD, that I am God.[Isa.43:2,3,5-7,12 KJV]. He that dwelleth in the secret place of the most High shall abide under the shadow of the Almighty. I will say of the LORD, He is my refuge and my fortress: my God; in him will I trust. Surely he shall deliver thee from the snare of the fowler, and from the noisome pestilence. He shall cover thee with his feathers, and under his wings shalt thou trust: his truth shall be thy shield and buckler. Thou shalt not be afraid for the terror by night; nor for the arrow that flieth by day.[Psalm 91:1-5 KJV].

REFLECTION:

_____

_____

_____

_____

_____

_____

_____

_____

_____

_____

_____

_____

_____

_____

_____

_____

_____

_____

_____

_____

_____

_____

Printed in the United States
By Bookmasters